D0396975

N

GALILEE

○ Sepphoris
○ Nazareth
○ Naim

RIVER JORDAN

SAMARIA

Sichar ○

PERAEA

PERSIA

JUDEA

Jericho ○

Jerusalem ⚓
○ Bethany
Bethlehem ★ ○ Marsaba

▲ MT. NEBO

SALT
(DEAD)
SEA

E A

HARRY SCOTT

Carole Florence Villanueva

The day Christ was born

A Reverential Reconstruction

ILLUSTRATED

THE
DAY
CHRIST
by Jim Bishop
WAS
BORN

HARPER & BROTHERS · NEW YORK

THE DAY CHRIST WAS BORN

COPYRIGHT © 1959, 1960 BY JIM BISHOP

PRINTED IN THE UNITED STATES OF AMERICA

All rights in this book are reserved. No part of the book may be used or reproduced in any manner whatsoever without written permission except in the case of brief quotations embodied in critical articles and reviews. For information address Harper & Brothers, 49 East 33rd Street, New York 16, N. Y.

Quotations from The New Testament, *translated by James A. Kleist, S.J., and Joseph L. Lilly, C.M. Copyright, 1954, by The Bruce Publishing Company.*

The black-and-white photographs credited to Matson Photo Service published by permission of The Matson Photo Service, Los Angeles, California.

Dedicated to Ralph Gorman, C.P., my mentor

The Illustrations

The great paintings reproduced in this book are of course not literal renditions, but they are faithful to the spirit of the story. The picture on the front of the jacket is a detail from "The Nativity," by Botticelli (1444/5–1510), which now hangs in the National Gallery, London.

An eight-page section of photographs showing the Holy Land today appears after page 52.

For the record

Nothing is known of the birth of Christ beyond the New Testament. It is a great and joyful story, the happiest event since the dawn of history. It needs no gilding. Still, there is a natural curiosity in the heart of the journalist to know more. He would like to fill in the blank spaces of any great event.

This one happened two thousand years ago. The town and the terrain of Bethlehem have not changed. The road down the Jordan Valley from Nazareth is a little smoother now, but it twists beside the same bank of the same river. The walls of Jerusalem have been moved in a little, especially on the south side, but the view of the Mount of Olives is the same, and Gethsemani still reposes at the base of the mountain.

The marriage customs of the Jews of two thousand years ago are recorded. The manner of courtship, to which Joseph and Mary surely subscribed, is also known. The cave where animals were sheltered beneath the inn at Bethlehem is still there. The facts about the Magi, as a class of philosophic astrologers, are available to those who seek them. In addition, there are ageless works written by scholars about the birth of Jesus.

I have availed myself of these things. The result is within these pages. Although the facts are as I present them, the book must be called a re-creation because it contains dialogue and minor scenes which are not to be found within the historical framework of the New Testament. These are my imaginings.

JIM BISHOP

Sea Bright, New Jersey

The day Christ was born

THE ROAD OUT OF BETHANY
threw a tawny girdle around the hill they called the
Mount of Olives and the little parties came up slowly
out of the east leading asses with dainty dark feet toward
the splendor of Jerusalem. They came up all year long
from Jericho and the Salt Sea and the Mountains of
Moab and the north country of Samaria and Galilee in
a never-ending procession to the great temple of Solomon.
It was a spiritual spawning; a coming home; a communion with God at his appointed house.

Joseph had never seen such awesome beauty. The elders

in Nazareth had described it as a rare white jewel set in the green valley between Kidron and Golgotha and he had asked questions about it but the elders—and his father too— seemed to lose themselves in arm waving and superlatives. Now he would see it. He reached the rise of the road, his feet tired and dirty from ninety miles of walking, and he unconsciously pulled the jackass a little faster.

"Are you quiet?" he said. His bride, called Miriam in the Aramean tongue, and Mary in others, jogged sideways on the little animal, and said that she was quiet. She felt no pain. This was the fifth day from Nazareth and, from hour to hour, she had progressed from tiredness to fatigue to weariness to the deep anesthesia of exhaustion. She felt nothing. She no longer noticed the chafe of the goatskin against her leg, nor the sway of the food bag on the other side of the animal. Her veiled head hung and she saw millions of pebbles on the road moving by her brown eyes in a blur, pausing, and moving by again with each step of the animal.

Sometimes she felt ill at ease and fatigued, but she swallowed this feeling and concentrated on what a beautiful baby she was about to have and kept thinking about it, the bathing, the oils, the feeding, the tender pressing of the tiny body against her breast—and the sickness went away. Sometimes she murmured the ancient prayers and, for the moment, there was no road and no pebbles and she dwelt on the wonder of God and saw him in a fleecy cloud at a windowless wall of an inn or a hummock of trees, walking backward in front of her husband, beckoning him on. God was everywhere. It gave Mary confidence to know that He was everywhere. She needed confidence. Mary was fifteen.

Most young ladies of the country were betrothed at thirteen and married at fourteen. A few were not joined in holiness until fifteen or sixteen and these seldom found a choice man and were content to be shepherds' wives, living in caves in the sides of the hills, raising their children in loneliness, knowing only the great stars of the night lifting over the hills, and the whistle of the shepherd as he turned to lead his flock to a new pasture. Mary had married a carpenter. He had been apprenticed by his father at bar mitzvah. Now he was nineteen and had his own business.

It wasn't much of a business, even for the Galilean country. He was young and, even though he was earnest to the point of being humorless, he was untried and was prone to mistakes in his calculations. In all of Judea there was little lumber. Some stately cedars grew in the powdery alkaline soil, but, other than date palms and fig trees and some fruit orchards, it was a bald, hilly country. Carpentry was a poor choice.

A rich priest might afford a house of wood, but most of the people used the substance only to decorate the interior. The houses were of stone, cut from big deposits eighteen inches under the topsoil. It was soft, when first exposed to air, and could be cut with wooden saws into cubes. These were staggered in courses to make a wall. Windows were small and placed high on each wall, so that, daily, squares of sunlight walked slowly across the earthen floor. Mary's house, like the average, was small and set against a hill in Nazareth. At the front, there was a stone doorsill. Over it hung a cloth drape. To enter, the drape was pushed aside.

The interior consisted of two rooms. The front one was Joseph's shop. In it were the workbench, the saws, the auger, the awl and hammers. There were clean-smelling boards and blond curls of shavings on the floor. In the back room there was an earthen oven to the left, three feet wide, six feet long and two feet high. The cooking was done in the stone-lined interior. The family slept on the earthen top of the oven. On chilly nights, the heat seeped through to warm the sleepers. To the right of the room was a table. There were no chairs because only rich Jews sat to eat, and they had learned this from traveling Greeks. Next to the table was a wooden tether for the ass. He was a member of the family, a most important member because he did the carrying of the raw lumber and the finished products, and he was also the sole means of transportation.

He was petted and loved and spoken to. On the tether, he watched Mary go about her duties. He flicked the flies from his ears and sometimes, when he tired of watching, his eyes closed and he locked his knees so that he would not fall, and he slept standing up. He was not a stubborn animal. He was most patient and he would stand while Joseph burdened him with a mound of objects. When the bridle strap was pulled by his master, the ass lowered his head, switched his tail against his flanks, and started off, the little hoofs making sounds like an inverted cup dropped in the mud.

This was the winter solstice of the Jewish year 3790.

The gaiety of the Feast of Chanukah had ended as Joseph and his wife left Nazareth. They had come down through Naim and on down into the valley of the Jordan. It was hot along the valley floor, but the Jews of the upland country seldom risked travel by the direct route through Samaria and Sichar, where the people at the village wells were unfriendly and argumentative.

Each night, when the sun was gone and the road obscure, Joseph led the ass a little way off from the river, away from the road and into a clearing where there was very little brush and few insects. Then he tied the ass, tilted the goatskin and filled the earthen jar with water from it, and sat. There was not much to talk about. Their minds were troubled with momentous events far beyond the scope of their thought; far beyond the rationalization of two simple peasants of the family of David. On the few occasions when they discussed it, both Mary and Joseph became overwhelmed and shy. They lapsed into silences and Joseph would mend the conversational rip with a question about Mary's family.

Mary was big with the baby, and awkward, but she managed to fetch the food and the bread from the pouch on the near side of the donkey, and to set it down as neatly and as appetizingly as possible. There was no meat. Even at home, they never had meat more than once a month. Mostly it was lamb, chopped into cubes and roasted and then set on a plate beside charoseth and other herbs and fruits.

They slept in the open, saving what little money they had for the day of the baby. Sometimes, when there was no moon, Joseph set the lamp on the ground and Mary removed her veil and brushed the long dark hair which hung to her waist. She said that she would like to bathe in the Jordan, and she said it wistfully because she knew that Joseph would say no, and a good wife did not dispute the will of her husband. On these occasions he said no. He said it gently, reminding her that her time was near, that this would be her first-born, and he would not assume the risk of the river. To this Mary made no reply. Joseph, touched with tenderness, said gruffly that the best he could do was to take some cloths to the Jordan, wet them and wring them out, and bring them to her. Mary said that she would appreciate it.

In the morning, with the sun still behind the Mountains of Moab, Joseph arose, adjusted his tunic, and fed the animal. He worked quietly, whispering to the jackass, setting the folded blanket behind the withers, adjusting and balancing the goatskin and the food bag, before awakening his wife. He felt an enormous compassion for this girl, but he could never explain it. Not even to himself. He had once felt this way toward a little boy who had a withered foot.

The road was busy at dawn. Sometimes Joseph had to wait until he could find room between parties going south. The road, it seemed, was always alive. The rich Greeks traveled south out of Sepphoris in sedan chairs, the servants shouldering the yokes easily and walking steadily, en route to Jerusalem to trade with the rich Jews. The northbound traffic came from Jerusalem and also from as far away as Egypt, and these merchants were laden with fabrics and metal objects and expensive spices. They left their elegant good wishes on the air behind them.

On the evening of the fourth day they were at Jericho, a few miles above the Salt Sea and within glance of Mt. Nebo to the east. Joseph wanted to stay at an inn, where they could pay for space on the floor, but Mary begged him not to do it. "This is not an important day," she said. He knew what she meant.

"One does not see a great place like Jericho often," he said softly. "It will be just as well if we eat at an inn and, as you say, sleep in the fields." He looked away. "I was thinking of you."

They ate at an inn on the far side of town, near where the wilderness begins. It was an ordinary place, catering to transients. It was a stone place, and one had to eat whatever the house offered. The food came in gleaming bowls, and Mary admitted to herself that it was better than anything she had to offer so, conversationally, she shifted the attack.

"There are many people in these places," she said.

Joseph shrugged. "A public house," he said. He was a medium-sized man with deep brown curls hanging to his shoulders. The hair was thick and parted in the middle. His beard was thin and scraggly, but he wiped it with his hand as though it were full. This, Mary understood, was natural in a young man.

She ate leaning against a wall. She said it made her back feel good. He stood flanking her, a wall of protection against the crush of people entering and leaving the place, babbling as though this were the last chance to inflict their opinions on others.

"It is better together," she said shyly.

"When we must eat in the fields," he said, "we will eat in the fields. This eating is rare."

Mary ate well, stealing furtive glances at Joseph and wondering what she did to deserve all the tumult of happiness she felt when he was near. It was like a tame storm in her heart, a relaxation of caution accompanied by the excitement of knowing that she belonged to this growing boy. She had never been anywhere, except to visit old relatives, and now, in advanced pregnancy, she was seeing much and knowing much in a few days.

In the morning, Joseph led Mary and the ass into the wilderness. It was twenty miles to Bethany, and, from there, three to the heart of Jerusalem. A man with strong legs could walk it, leading an animal and a woman, before sundown. The wilderness is a barren place in the mountains, where nothing of consequence grows and the tiny peaks look alike, ochre and white and chalky, a place where bandits await the ornate sedan chairs and the sun smites the walker until the sweat itches his legs and softens the straps of his sandals.

Joseph stopped at the top of the rise. The ass stopped,

and used a hind leg to kick the flies from the underside of his belly. Mary looked up, a tired child with eyes partly conscious of the scene.

"Jerusalem," Joseph said, pointing. She looked. The wonderment of what she saw caused the nausea to fade. Her eyes lost the glazed look. She had heard her father describe this place when she was a little girl. A glance told her that the poor man did not know how to make anyone see Jerusalem. Joseph opened his mouth to speak, but what his eyes saw made his mind drunk and paralyzed his tongue.

It was a thing to see. The late sun was ahead, across the hill behind Jerusalem. The city was a white jewel pronged by the great stone wall around it. Joseph pulled the ass to the side of the road because the pilgrims behind him were shouting. Without turning from the scene, he moved back along the flank of the ass until he touched Mary's hand. "Jerusalem," he said again. He said it as though it were an earthly anteroom to paradise, as indeed it was.

The sun would be gone in ten minutes and there was much to see because he could not stay in Jerusalem. His destination, Bethlehem, was still five miles to the south, but he did not mind the night walk if he could stop a moment and drink in all of this and remember it when he was old.

His eyes, and Mary's too, moved in little darting glances, and they longed to exclaim to each other but there were no words. This was where God lived. They had been told many times that he did not live in the little synagogues around the country of Judea and far out in the diaspora. The synagogues were there to remind the Jews of God, to remind them of their duty never to live more than ninety days travel from the Great Temple of Jerusalem, never to fail, whenever possible, to go to Jerusalem for the Passover. Each year at the time of the first seder, 300,000 Jews stayed in the city and in the hilly fields around it.

Below was the Valley of Kidron, with the full little river running cold below the east wall of the temple. Gray-blue smoke hung still in the sky over the temple proper. This was the last sacrifices of the day, the last baby lambs on the altar. Inside, there were seven thousand Levitical priests to ascertain that each lamb, before sacrifice, was without blemish, and in the courtyards to the north were animals and birds to be bought for sacrifice.

The Porch of Solomon faced them, the marble walk and corinthian columns gleaming like teeth in a seven-foot mouth. Up the side of the great temple was the snowy stone wall, hung with a cluster of solid gold grapes four stories high. In the valley, the Golden Gate and the Fountain Gate slowly regurgitated the last of the temple pilgrims for the day. From the height, Joseph could look across the enclosed city and see Herod's palace on the far side, a little south of the place called Galgotha.

Softly, haltingly, Joseph found his voice and, as he drank in the exquisite and almost fearful beauty, he began to tell the story to his wife. She knew the story as well as he, but she listened dutifully, interjecting a word here and there, or a question. He reminded her that he came of the family of David, even though his branch was small and poor. It was David's son Solomon who had built this. He had commissioned Hiram, the King of Tyre, to draw the plans and do the engineering. The work was finished in seven years, a miracle of goodness. The temple was on Ornan's Rock. It was 1,600 feet long and 970 feet wide. The bigger the temple got, the more remote Solomon felt from God, and he needed the solace of women, so on the

Mount of Offense to the left he had built a palace and placed therein five hundred concubines.

The sin needed washing and, long after Solomon repented, the Jews split into two nations—Judea and Israel —and the Babylonians defeated them and reduced the walls of the temple. Now the Jews were the chattels of Roman emperors and the Caesars appointed Herod as king to rule the people.

The Herod who sat in that palace on the far side of the city proclaimed himself a Jew and made daily sacrifices, but he was not even a good hypocrite. Joseph had heard the elders talk about it in Nazareth, and they averted their eyes when they recited his crimes. Herod bent his knee to Rome. He married Mariamne and, after she bore him two sons, he became piqued and had the three slain. He married ten times and he was so cruel that Caesar Augustus in Rome said that it was safer to be Herod's pig than Herod's son. This was a sacrilegious joke on the dietary laws, and Joseph did not like to repeat it.

Still—how could one say it?—he had also done good things for God. He had paid ten thousand workmen to repair the temple and rebuild the walls of Jerusalem. He

made temple spires of marble and they glinted pink in the
morning sun. He built a great outer portico around the
temple and this was called the Court of the Gentiles. Non-
believers could walk this far. The next inner walk was
called the Court of the Women, then came the Court
of the Israelite Men. Signs proclaimed that any non-
believer who walked this far in the temple was liable to
death.

Then came the smaller Court of Priests, and inside of it
the temple itself. This consisted of two huge chambers.
The outer was the Holy; the inner was the Holy of Holies.
In front of the Holy was a heavy veil embroidered in rich
color, with all the known flowers of the earth, and a vari-
ety of the fruits of the earth.

"Darkness is upon us," said Mary. She had a feeling of
foreboding. She wanted to proceed to Bethlehem for no
reason other than that she was trembling and the baby
was unusually quiet. Joseph stopped in mid-speech. He
knew that she would not interrupt him unless there was a
reason. He asked if she desired to get down and have privacy. She said no and, without further conversation, he
led the ass westward into the valley and across the little
wooden bridge over the Kidron and beneath the great

wall of the city and then by the Valley of Hinnon and on up into the hills between Jerusalem and Bethlehem.

It was soon night and moonless. Joseph trod slowly, stumbling on stones underfoot, and wondering how much of a man he would be if brigands sprang out of the dark. There was little traffic on the road; a few transients who lived near Jerusalem hurried by, trying to reach home without spending an extra night under the stars.

Something happened suddenly to Mary and she knew in a moment that this would be the night of the baby. She asked Joseph to stop and he became alarmed and asked if she was unquiet. "No," she said. "I feel no pain, but we must find an inn. The baby—with God's help— will be born tonight."

Joseph was frightened. He knew nothing of these things.

The thinking Mary did about the events leading to this night was a kaleidoscope of happy and mysterious and supernatural things calculated to unnerve the most serene young lady. To have a first baby is, in itself, a towering, wordless joy, a living proof of the most common miracle, a sad tenderness to constrict the heart and mist the eyes. To give birth to a first-born who is God and the Son of

God and the Second Person of the Holy Trinity is, at age fifteen or any greater age, a heavier responsibility than any other person ever bore, an enormity of weight which could be maintained only by one too young to appreciate it.

MARY WAS BORN AND RAISED in Nazareth, the child of an average family. She played on the streets, as the other children did, and she was subject to parental discipline. Joseph knew her, even though he was four years older. All houses in Nazareth were in the same neighborhood because it was a small town. The biggest event that could occur in Nazareth was for a father to take his children to the nearby Greek city of Sepphoris to shop in the bazaars. The people were knit closely in their daily lives, and the women met in the morning at the village well.

When Mary reached her thirteenth birthday, it was permissible to ask for her in marriage. The proper form was followed. Joseph first asked his parents if he could marry Mary. He was seventeen, an apprentice carpenter in the neighborhood and more than a year away from having his own shop. It was assumed that a serious-minded young Jew of seventeen was a responsible adult.

Joseph's parents discussed the matter of marriage and, in time, paid a formal call on Mary's parents. The entire neighborhood knew in advance what negotiations were at hand, and, from draped doorway to draped doorway, the women discussed it as they washed the stones in front of their houses. Mary was not supposed to know of the matter, but had *ex facto* knowledge of it all along and had made known her wishes to her mother and father. Joseph, who thought it was a deep, pending secret, was amazed and embarrassed to find that the boss carpenter and the tradesmen were not only aware of his wishes, but looked at him archly, stroked their beards, and made him the butt of unsmiling jests.

The parents engaged in their formal discussion. It was necessary, as part of the little ceremonial, to talk of a

PINACOTECA COMUNALE, CITTA DI CASTELLO

The Annunciation
Andrea della Robbia (1435–1525?)

MUSEE ROYAL DES BEAUX-ARTS, BRUSSELS

The Census in Bethlehem (*detail*)
Pieter Bruegel the Elder (ca. 1525/30–1569)

dowry, but Mary's people had none. Their economic status was no better, no worse, than Joseph's: as long as the man of the house remained in good health, they would not starve.

When the two mothers and two fathers were agreed, the qiddushin took place. This is a formal betrothal, and much more binding than any other. The qiddushin has the finality of marriage. Once the marriage contract was negotiated, even though the marriage ceremony had not occurred, the bridegroom-to-be could not be rid of his betrothed except through divorce. The qiddushin, in Judea, also entitled the couple to lawful sexual relations, even though each of the parties was still living at home with his parents. However, in the country of Galilee and in the south, the people had renounced the privilege more than five hundred years before, and purity was maintained through the final marriage vows.

Still, if Joseph had died between qiddushin and marriage, Mary would have been his legal widow. If, in the same period, another man had had knowledge of her, Mary would have been punished as an adulteress. The waiting time was spent, according to custom, in shopping for a small home and furniture. The nissu'in, or wedding ceremony, would be almost anticlimactic. A big part of the ceremony was the solemn welcome of the bridegroom to his bride at the door of his new home.

Throughout the engagement, Mary, of course, lived with her parents and accepted the daily chores set out for her. At a time midway between engagement and formal marriage, Mary was alone one day and was visited by the angel Gabriel. She was alarmed, to be sure, but not as frightened as she would have been had she not heard stories of such visits from the elders. Mary lived after the days of the great prophets, the great visions, the visitations.

Gabriel stood before her and saw a dark, modest child of fourteen. "Rejoice, child of grace," he said. "The Lord is your helper. You are blessed beyond all women." Mary did not like the sound of the last sentence. Her hands began to shake. Why should she, a little country girl, be blessed beyond all women? Did it mean that she was about to die? Was she being taken, perhaps, to a far-off place, never again to see her mother and her father and—and— Joseph?

She said nothing. She tried to look away, not only because of terror but because it was considered bad manners in Judea for one to stare directly into the eyes of another, but her eyes were magnetized. She stared, and lowered her eyes, and stared again.

Gabriel's voice softened. "Do not tremble, Mary," he said. "You have found favor in the eyes of God. Behold: you are to be a mother and to bear a son, and to call him Jesus. He will be great: 'Son of the Most High' will be his title, and the Lord God will give to him the throne of his father, David. He will be king over the house of Jacob forever, and to his kingship there will be no end."

The words did not calm Mary. Vaguely, she understood that she was to be the mother of a king of kings, but who might this be and how could it occur when she was not even married?

"How will this be," she said shyly, "since I remain a virgin?"

It was Gabriel's turn to become specific. He stood in soft radiance in the room and explained. "The Holy Spirit will come upon you, and the power of the Most High will overshadow you. For this reason the child to be born will be acclaimed 'Holy' and 'Son of God.' " She now understood the words, but they added to her bewilderment. What the angel was saying, she reasoned, was something for which the Jews had been waiting for centuries: a messiah, a saviour, God come to earth as he had promised long ago. Mary shook her head.

Not to her. Not to her.

Gabriel sensed that the child needed more proof. "Note, moreover," he said, "your relative Elizabeth, in her old age, has also conceived a son and is now in her sixth month—she who was called 'The barren.' Nothing indeed is impossible for God."

Her eyes lowered to the earthen floor, and her head inclined too. She comprehended. She also understood that the angel had told her about her old cousin Elizabeth, whom she had not seen in some time, so that the fruitfulness of her kinswoman would be the earthly seal of proof to the heavenly words. She, a young virgin, was to be blessed by the Holy Spirit and she would bear a male child who would be God. It was an enormous honor, but she had been taught to accept and obey the will of God from the first moments of early understanding.

"Regard me as the humble servant of the Lord," she

murmured. "May all that you have said be fulfilled in me."

The angel stood before her in silence, fading slowly from her vision, bit by bit, until all that was visible was the wall. Mary's impulse was to run and find her mother. She must tell. She must ask counsel. She must convince her mother that she was not inventing a story. Exultation came and it was transmuted to anguish. It was not a dream. Or was it? Could one dream, standing wide awake in one's house?

No, it was not a dream. She knew that it could not be, because she could not have devised the words that Gabriel used. Now, for a moment, she had trouble remembering them. She wrung her hands and prayed for recollection. Full recollection. She had to know every word and, more important, to understand every word. She prayed and thought and prayed and, little by little, the words and phrases returned until, like a familiar litany, she could recite them without hesitation.

She thought again of her mother and decided not to tell. If the angel had wanted her mother to know, he would have come when her mother was at home, so that both of them would have had knowledge of this thing. He had deliberately selected a time when she was alone. Therefore, it must be the will of God that she keep the secret. Anyway, if her mother or anyone else knew the secret, they would tell it to her, and thus she would know which human beings God had selected to know of the honor.

Surely, she thought, Joseph would know. He was her intended husband. The angel would have to tell Joseph. If he didn't, then what would Joseph think when she became great with child and he knew that the baby was not his? Oh yes, the angel would surely tell Joseph.

Within a few days, Mary asked, as casually as possible, for permission to visit her cousin Elizabeth. Her mother thought of it as a touching sign of devotion, and sent her off with a family traveling south to Judea. The young virgin said nothing about her secret. Some of the time she seemed to her friends to be lost in a frowning reverie.

Elizabeth was gray and wrinkled, and she had spent many years in the balcony of the synagogue asking God for a child. Her husband, Zachary, was a priest, a small-town teacher who had once been selected by the great priests of Jerusalem to be the one to enter the holy place and offer the incense. He felt sorrier for his Elizabeth than he did for himself in the matter of childlessness. He understood the natural maternal feelings of Elizabeth and, unknown to her, he had prayed again and again for a child.

Sometime before the visit of Mary, the angel Gabriel had appeared before the old lady and told her that God had answered her prayers. She would give birth to a son in June, and she must call him John. Someday in the distant future he would be called the Baptist, and he would go ahead of the messiah, preaching and baptizing as he went. The angel told Elizabeth more. Much more.

Elizabeth was standing in her doorway as Mary came up the walk. It was as though she had expected the visit. Mary, an affectionate child, shouted a happy greeting before she reached the door. Elizabeth felt her baby move within her and, in raising her hand in greeting, suddenly burst into tears. "Blessed are you," she said, "beyond all women. And blessed is the fruit of your womb!"

Mary stopped, part way to the door. Her mouth hung open. She could not speak. Elizabeth knew! Elizabeth knew the secret! Elizabeth wiped her eyes and tried to smile. "How privileged am I," she said to her niece, "to have the mother of my Lord come to visit me. Hear me now: as the sound of your greeting fell upon my ears, the babe in my womb leaped for joy! Happy is she who believed that what was told her on behalf of the Lord would be fulfilled."

The last sentence was a quasi-warning for the young girl to erase all doubt from her mind, and become reconciled to the greatest duty of all ages. Mary had not doubted. She had believed the words, but she could not convince herself that she was the one, of all women on earth, selected to bear the Baby. Now she was convinced. She no longer tried to divorce her person from the prophecy. She had told no one of the secret, and here Aunt Elizabeth not only knew about it, but was pregnant exactly as the angel had said she would be.

A wave of exultation filled the heart of Mary. The young girl no longer wondered and worried about her part in God's will. She became lyrical and she stood before her aunt, arms outstretched, eyes dimmed and half-closed with tears of joy, and she uttered words which remained engraved on the heart of Elizabeth for all days:

"My soul extols the Lord;
and my spirit leaps for joy in God my saviour.
How graciously He looked upon this lowly maid!
Oh, behold, from this hour onward
age after age will call me blessed!
How sublime is what He has done for me—
the Mighty One, whose name is 'Holy.'
From age to age He visits those
who worship Him in reverence.
His arm achieves the mastery:
He routes the haughty and proud of heart;
He puts down princes from their thrones,
and exalts the lowly;
He fills the hungry with blessings,
and sends away the rich with empty hands.
He has taken by the hand His servant Israel,
and mercifully kept His faith
—as He had promised our fathers—
with Abraham and his posterity
forever and evermore."

The women embraced and Mary wondered what made
her think of those words. The young girl remained with

Elizabeth until June, a week prior to the birth of John. Mary was three months pregnant and her parents had sent word that she should be at home preparing for her wedding. Yes, the wedding. Elizabeth now enjoyed Mary's complete confidence and the two wondered if Joseph knew. It was important that he know what was about to happen, and to understand.

When Mary arrived home, she saw her husband-to-be. He was not happy that she had chosen to be away from him for three months and, if he knew the secret, he hid it well. He had heard from Mary's mother that Elizabeth was to bear a child, but surely there were others in her town who could have attended her. The young girl did not dispute Joseph. She decided, from his attitude, that he knew nothing of the great secret. She would not marry him without telling something of it.

"I'm going to have a baby," she said. The shock to Joseph was beyond measure. Throughout the courtship, his intended bride had worn an aura of innocence; he was painfully conscious of her lack of knowledge. She had gone away three months ago, and now she returned to say that she was pregnant.

It is impossible to read the depths of sorrow in both

hearts. He looked at her tenderly and she offered no word of explanation. She looked away from him and wished that she might tell everything. The baby was going to need a foster father—who better than the man she loved, the gentle and pious and patient Joseph? The thought crossed her mind that he had been selected for the role for these very reasons. He would be an ideal guardian for the infant. Then why, why had he not been told? Why wrench two young hearts with tragedy when the truth was as bright as the sun and as warming?

On the tip of her tongue Mary had the greatest secret of all history. She could not unlock her tongue. Joseph went away from her to think. Of the two, he was the more pitiable. He loved this girl with all his heart and he had had visions of a long and fruitful life with her. Now, he felt, she had betrayed him and he could not understand the betrayal, nor even force himself to believe that it was true.

Joseph kept his awful secret. He could divorce her publicly. If he did this, he would be impelled to tell the elders the reason. In that case, they would ask Mary if she was with child. If she said yes, Joseph would have to swear that he was "without knowledge of her." The priests would adjudge her to be an adulteress. There was only one penalty for this crime: stoning. The guilty person is led by townsmen to a high cliff and ordered to jump. If the adulteress refuses, she is pushed. As she lies at the bottom of the cliff, the people arm themselves with stones, and watch. If she moves, they throw the stones. If she doesn't, they go home. The body is left where it is for the birds and the animals.

Joseph was being put to a test. He did not want Mary to die. He loved her. He could, under the law, pay money to put her away, to have her sent to some remote place. There, she could have her baby and remain. A third possibility would be for Joseph to swallow his pride, proceed with the wedding, and hope that there would not be too much comment in the town over a six-month baby.

He was dwelling upon the possibilities one night in bed. Suddenly, the carpenter made up his mind. He would put Mary away privately. It would break his heart, and he knew that he could not love anyone else, but it would be just and, at the same time, merciful.

Within a few moments after the decision was reached,

relaxation came to Joseph, and he slept. In sleep, he was visited by an angel. The spirit said to him "Joseph, son of David, do not scruple to take Mary, your wife, into your home. Her conception was wrought by the Holy Spirit. She will bear a son and you are to name him Jesus; for he will save his people from their sins."

When Joseph awakened, he remembered the dream and he wondered if his forlorn hopes were reaching for rationalization. A dream was nothing more than a dream. His unconscious wishes might be fulfilled in sleep. Still, if this were so, he would never dream a blasphemy in which the pregnancy was excused by attributing it to God. Besides, the dream fulfilled an old prophecy to the letter: "Behold, the virgin will be pregnant and give birth to a son, who will be called 'Emmanuel,' which means 'God with us.' "

Joseph felt refreshed. He felt happy. The more he dwelt upon the dream, the more clearly he saw the hand of God revealing a great truth to him. It required restraint to go to work, making stalls and tables and wooden hangers for utensils and closets for garments. He longed to hurry to Mary's house, yelling: "I know! I know!" His patience manifested itself, and he waited until the proper time, after supper, and when she saw his first glance, Mary knew that he knew before he took her for an evening walk to explain.

God had tried both of these young people, and they had not failed him. Still, Joseph was worried because he did not understand what part he was to play, nor how best to interpret the will of God. The scripture plainly said that the messiah would be born of a virgin, and Joseph interpreted this to mean that he would have no prerogatives as a husband, now or ever. The following week, they were married and Joseph took Mary to his home. One of his worries, he confided to Mary, was that if the old prophecy of a messiah was to be fulfilled, then something was wrong because everyone knew that the sacred scriptures said that the King of Kings would be born in Bethlehem—the City of David. Their infant would be born in Nazareth, a little place over ninety miles north of Bethlehem.

She had no intention of traveling anywhere, Mary said. She was going to remain here in Nazareth. In the summer months, and the early autumn, the older women of the town noticed that she was pregnant, and they counseled her to remain close to her home. She would not go to see

Elizabeth's baby, so why would she consider traveling to Bethlehem? Joseph nodded. That was the way he felt. He had never been to Bethlehem and he had no intention of going there.

IN ROME, CAESAR AUGUSTUS learned that many of his subjects were dishonest. He ruled the known world, but the amount of taxes was not commensurate with the number of subjects. He held a council in Rome, and his advisors told Caesar that he could not levy an equitable tax until he had an accurate idea of the populations of the several provinces.

Caesar issued an imperial rescript ordering all subjects, in the winter solstice, to return to the cities of their fathers and there be counted. This, of course, would work hardship on millions of people, and in a two-week period of migration would upset the economic balance as men left their work to travel to distant cities, but it had to be done. The census would be taken in many tongues, and in places along the Rhine River, the Danube, in North Africa, Portugal, Syria, Belgium, Egypt, Palestine and all along the north Mediterranean shore.

Many of the subject people chafed when the law was proclaimed. They said that Caesar was not a just king to do this to them. Even in a small town like Nazareth, which Caesar Augustus would not know by name, the Jews said that it was not fair. Joseph sought the local tax merchant and asked if women in advanced pregnancy could be excused and he was told that no one could be excused. Even the lame and the blind had to report to the cities of their fathers, and many would have to be carried on pallets.

Joseph consoled Mary by telling her that the ancient prophecy, in spite of their wishes, was coming true. She saw the truth of this and her murmurs of discontent died on her lips. Originally, she had protested that a long, rough journey would risk the life of the baby. On second thought, this appeared to be a ridiculous assumption because, if she had been graced by God to bear the messiah, then nothing could happen to the baby.

They started on the trip south, two young and solemn people with a short and slender jackass who bore the most exalted burden ever to honor an animal. Joseph lifted Mary's spirits by reminding her that, if he paced the trip correctly, and they were not halted by heavy rains or sandstorms, she would see Jerusalem at sundown of the 5th day.

The final few miles were fatiguing. Joseph stumbled many times in the dark and, over his shoulder, he asked his wife if she was quiet. When they were two miles from Bethlehem, she said no. She felt uncomfortable, she said, but it was bearable and she had no complaint. She hoped that they would reach the inn in time.

The stretch of road into Bethlehem curved broadly and climbed steadily. To the left the valley was precipitous. Four hundred feet below, the whistle of shepherds could be heard and sometimes, in the deep silences, the shepherds could be heard exchanging greetings. It was a cool night with a fair breeze coming out of the south. In the darkness, the stars brightened and swelled so that, among the clusters of little blue ones, big ones winked coldly across the centuries of time.

Joseph leaned forward to pull the ass a little faster. He reached the city of David and found, to his dismay, that there were multitudes of people, some sleeping beside the road. He had not realized that there were so many who belonged to the House of David. His heart sank as he found that Bethlehem consisted of one main road running north and south, and two cross streets. The inn was to the left, built on a cliff of rocky soil overlooking the valley. Joseph went directly to the inn, knowing that he would find room there or he would find it nowhere.

He left Mary and the animal outside, and assured his wife that he would make arrangements. She too could see the crowds. Some families were sleeping outside the inn, against the wall. She said nothing. Joseph started to go inside, then stopped and returned.

"Under the law," he said, "you must have a midwife at once. Let me first find one."

She shook her head no. The important thing, she said, was privacy. She was not worried about assistance. God had promised to take care of her, and she needed no additional help.

Joseph went inside. The floor of the main room was full of people sleeping in their clothing, with bundles propped under their heads. The odors of the unwashed, and spiced foods, filled the place. The young man sought the proprietor. With supplication on his face, he begged for a small private place for his wife, who was with child. The owner listened and threw up both hands. Where? he asked. Where would you go for privacy? His own family had no room in which to sleep. Every cubit of space had been rented three days ago, and some of the transients were taking turns sleeping in one space.

My wife, said Joseph in a tone this side of begging, is outside. She will have her first-born in an hour or two. Can you not please find room? A little room? The owner became irritable. Every house, every field in Bethlehem was filled with people from all over Judea. Some of the regular caravans between Egypt and the upland country chose to continue their journeys at night rather than remain in this overcrowded place. Where then could a woman have a baby? Nowhere. Some people were even sleeping below in the valley, skirted by bleating sheep looking for grass.

The owner's wife heard part of the plea. She called her husband aside and asked questions. The night was chill, she said. Look at the men outside the inn, sleeping with their cloaks over their noses. Why could not the young man take his wife to the cave below, the cave where the animals were kept?

The owner shrugged. If Joseph wanted privacy, he said, the only place left was down the side path to the cave where the asses and small animals were kept. The young man was welcome to it, if one wanted to bring a baby into the world in a place like that. Joseph inclined his head. "I am grateful," he said. "I thank you."

He dragged his feet returning to Mary. He told her the news. She was not vexatious; in fact, she seemed to be relieved. "Take me," she said. "The time grows short."

There were paths leading from both sides of the inn down the side of the cliff. In front, as on the bow of a big ship, there was an entrance to the cave, which had been carved out a long time ago. Joseph paused to light his small lamp, then led the donkey inside. He turned to look at Mary, and, in the yellow rays, he saw that she was in deep fatigue. The chalk of the road had powdered her face. She removed her veil, shook out her hair, and slid down off the animal. Her bones ached.

Joseph apologized. He said that he was sorry that the Hospice of Chamaan had no room for her, but she could see the crowds of people. He was ashamed that he had failed her in this hour. He must confess that he had not been much of a husband; he hadn't even found a midwife.

For a moment, Mary studied her husband. She brought a tender smile to her face. She told her husband that he had not failed her; he had been good and tender and lawful. He hung his head and listened. Mary looked around at the haltered cattle, the few lambs, some asses and a camel. If it is the will of God, she said, that His son should be born in a place like this, she would not question the wisdom of it.

At the age of fifteen, she would undergo this trial alone, just as, thirty-four years later, her son would undergo his trial alone. She asked Joseph to build a small fire on the path outside, and to fetch some water from the goatskin. Joseph did as she directed. He found an extra lamp hanging on a stable peg, he lit it and the stable brightened, and the animals watched in glistening-eyed silence, their breaths making small gray plumes in the gloom.

Joseph collected clean straw from the feed boxes, cleaned out a stall, and arranged the straw as a bed and placed his cloak over it. Then he looked for wood outside, and found none. He went back up to the hospice, and bought some charcoal from the owner. When the water was hot, he filled a jar, and brought it to Mary with some cloths. She was standing, hanging onto the wall of the stall with both hands.

Her head was down, and he could not see her face. In fear, he asked her to name what he could do. She said to go outside and tend the fire and heat more water and to remain there until she called him. The animals watched him go, and they watched impassively as Mary sank to the straw.

The fire outside burned brightly in the southerly breeze and little trains of ruddy sparks flew off into the dark night. Joseph sat beside it, heating the water and praying.

No one came down from the inn to ask how the young woman felt. If she prayed, no one heard except the animals, some of whom stopped chewing for a moment to watch; others of whom opened sleepy eyes to see. Time was slow; there was an infinity of silence; a timeless time when the future of mankind hung in empty space.

Joseph had run out of prayers and promises. His face was sick, his eyes listless. He looked up toward the east, and his dark eyes mirrored a strange thing: three stars, coming over the Mountains of Moab, were fused into one tremendously bright one. His eyes caught the glint of bright blue light, almost like a tiny moon, and he wondered about it and was still vaguely troubled by it when he heard a tiny, thin wail, a sound so slender that one had to listen again for it to make sure.

He wanted to rush inside at once. He got to his feet, and he moved no further. She would call him. He would wait. Joseph paced up and down, not realizing that men had done this thing for centuries before he was born, and would continue it for many centuries after he had gone.

"Joseph." It was a soft call, but he heard it. At once, he picked up the second jar of water and hurried inside. The two lamps still shed a soft glow over the stable, even though it seemed years since they had been lighted.

The first thing he noticed was his wife. Mary was sitting tailor-fashion with her back against a manger wall. Her face was clean; her hair had been brushed. There were blue hollows under her eyes. She smiled at her husband and nodded. Then she stood.

She beckoned him to come closer. Joseph, mouth agape, followed her to a little manger. It had been cleaned but, where the animals had nipped the edges of the wood, the boards were worn and splintered. In the manger were the broad bolts of white swaddling she had brought on the trip. They were doubled underneath and over the top of the baby.

Mary smiled at her husband as he bent far over to look. There, among the cloths, he saw the tiny red face of an infant. This, said Joseph to himself, is the one of whom the angel spoke. He dropped to his knees beside the manger. This was the messiah.

Down in the valley, sheep huddled against the chill. The shepherds sat on little eminences, dozing. The herds wandered by day, up and down the grasslands of Judea, always edging closer to Jerusalem, the big market for sheep. Those without blemish brought a good price as sacrificial animals for the temple. The others were sold for shearing and for food.

The people of the town scorned the shepherds. They were wanderers. They had no roots. They seldom married and, when they did, they stripped the soil from the hillsides, exposing the soft white rock beneath. The men carved apartments in these hills, and raised their families remote from the towns.

Some were dozing, a few were watching, when the deep

night sky was split with light. It was brighter than day, more like staring at a noon sun, and the sleeping shepherds awakened and, in fear, hid their eyes in the folds of their garments. After a moment, the intense light faded, and an angel appeared in bodily form, standing in air over the valley.

The herders were terrified and their sheep began to run in tight circles. "Do not fear," the angel said slowly, and the words seemed to echo off both sides of the valley of Bethlehem. Some of the men took heart and looked up. Some did not. "Listen," the angel said, "I bring you good news of great joy which is in store for the whole nation."

Good news? This would make any Jew open his eyes and lift them to the skies. They had been afraid of the justice and vengeance of God for centuries. They had worshiped carefully, with respect for all of the nuances of ritual, for fear that God might be displeased and visit unhappiness upon their people. Now—good news?

They looked up hopefully and the angel spoke again. The voice seemed to permeate the valley. "A saviour," the angel said, "who is the Lord Messias, was born to you today in David's town. And this will serve you as a token: you will find an infant wrapped in swaddling clothes and cradled in a manger."

The shepherds repeated the words. "A saviour . . . Lord Messias . . . David's town . . . infant in a manger." There was nothing frightening in that news. The angel had spoken correctly. It was good news. It was better than good news. It was the long-awaited news. It was the thing which had been promised by God a long time ago. It was the advent of him who would save the people of the world.

The dark brown eyes of the shepherds studied the angel and saw the effulgent light on the sheep and the rocky sides of the hills, and they knew that they were not sleeping. This thing was happening; happening to lonely and despised men in a valley beneath Bethlehem.

They were still dwelling on the wonders of God and his works when the angel was joined by hundreds of others, who appeared brightly in the night sky, and began to sing in a heavenly chorus:

"Glory to God in the heavens above,
and on earth peace to men of good will."

Slowly, the angels floated across the sky and disappeared. The shepherds approached each other in the darkness and asked: "What did you see?" "Did you hear as I heard?" "Is it true that the Son of God has come to save the twelve tribes of Israel?" "You are sure that this is not the work of some evil Egyptian magician who would steal our flocks?" They babbled awhile, and one said: "Let us go over to Bethlehem and find out the truth about this thing the Lord has made known to us."

Always, in times of crisis, the shepherds delegated a few of their number to guard the sheep. This time, in high excitement, they left in a group, confident that, in this moment of ecstasy, God would not permit their sheep to stray. They moved across the dark, grassy valley and up the sides of the hills, climbing and talking and wondering.

The older shepherds were certain that this was not a hoax. All Jews were good scriptural students and, because there were no common books, they memorized all their teachings about God. He had promised a saviour, and the great one would come of the House of David. This would be Bethlehem. The aspect which mystified all the shepherds was that the birth of the messiah was undignified.

One could not imagine the Son of God being born in a stable.

It had been said by the elders that when the saviour came to earth, he could be expected on a great white cloud, sitting in august kingliness, listening to the trumpets and songs of hosts of angels surrounding his throne as he ruled over heaven and earth. Tonight, the angels seemed to be an afterthought. It was as though his birth had been so insignificant, so humble, that the angels had to come down to summon a few lonely men to go to the stable and worship him.

A stable? God? Could he not at least have been born in the great palace of Herod the King? Or perhaps in the Holy of Holies of the great temple of Solomon? A manger, the angel said. They understood the word. It meant a sort of trough out of which animals ate grain. It would have the sweet odor of old oats and barley, and the sides would be chewed and chipped. A salt cake would lie in the bottom.

The shepherds reached the top of the eminence and walked among the dozing pilgrims of Bethlehem, asking where the messiah might be found. Most of the men turned away from them in silence. A few asked what messiah;

The Holy Land Today

BY BURTON HOLMES FROM EWING GALLOWAY

A view of Nazareth today.

JIM BISH

A panorama of the ageless Judean Hills. Mary and Joseph doubtless s
these same hills as they made their way to Jerusalem.

MATSON PHOTO SERVICE

Shepherds watching their flocks by night, as they have done for centuries. This photograph was taken on the Shepherds' Fields, and the faint outline of Bethlehem can be seen in the distance.

EWING GALLOWAY

View in the Nile Delta area, Egypt.

EWING GALLOWAY

A view of Bethlehem today.

JIM BISHOP

The main street of present-day Bethlehem, photographed by the author.

BY SCOFIELD FROM EWING GALLOWAY

The interior of the Crusader Church of the Nativity in Bethlehem. Beneath this spot is the cave in which Christ was born.

EWING GALLOWAY

"The road out of Bethany threw a tawny girdle around the hill they called the Mount of Olives. . . ."

MATSON PHOTO SERVICE

Evening over present-day Jerusalem, viewed from across the Kidron Valley. The building with the great dome in the center left of the photograph marks the site

the shepherds asked if anyone had seen the angels. What angels? Some of the wayfarers were rude: they asked the shepherds if they had become mad through too much grape.

Abuse was not unbearable or new to the herders. They had known it before. Patiently, they continued their rounds, asking here and there and finally confining their questions to this: Where can we find a newborn baby in this town? Someone told them to try the inn. The inn-keeper, exhausted with his labors, remembered the young man and pregnant young lady going to the cave beneath the inn.

The shepherds approached timidly. They moved down the path in their sandals, whispering. As they approached the lighted aperture, they crouched and coughed. Joseph came out. He studied them solemnly, without rancor, and the leaders told him that they had seen angels in the valley, and one angel had said that a messiah had been born this night in the town of David. They had—well, if it wasn't too soon—they had come to worship him.

Mary heard, and told Joseph to permit the men to come in. Joseph had some tools in his hand. His spouse told him that the nights would be too cold to permit the infant to travel until after the circumcision. They would have to continue to live in the stable for eight days. Joseph had gone into town and awakened a carpenter and explained the circumstances. Now he had tools and, with the permission of the owner of the inn, he was using sides of stalls to build a small, almost private room for his Mary and baby.

The shepherds came in, the cowls down off their heads. Their hair was long and ringleted, the beards trembled with murmured prayer, the hands were clasped piously before their chests. In the flickering yellow light of the oil lamp, they saw the child-mother, seated on straw. She was looking over the side of an old manger. The men lifted themselves a little on their toes to peer over the sides. Inside was an abundance of white swaddling clothes. An aura of light seemed to radiate from it.

Without looking up, the mother knew that they were trying to see her precious baby, so she stuck a finger into the white cloth and pulled it away from the infant's face. The men looked, with mouths open, and fell to their knees. They adored the baby, and thanked him for coming to save the nation. They recited some of the formal prayers. Joseph, standing aside, was amazed that so many strangers now knew the secret.

The shepherds were torn between wonderment and happiness. This little baby was God and the Son of God, but he was also a helpless, lovable infant. Their hearts welled with joy and the stern, deeply bronzed faces kept melting into big grins, which were quickly erased as the sheep men recalled that they were in the presence of the King of All Kings.

The scene in a chilly manger, warmed by the bodies and breathing of the animals, was, to the shepherds, closer to their hearts than if the messiah had come on a big cloud with trumpeting angels. They understood babies, and they understood animals and they murmured with delight that God would see fit to come to earth in an abode only slightly less worthy than their own homes in the hills.

They remained kneeling, clasping and unclasping their hands, and staring at the face of the infant, as though trying to etch on their memories the peaceful scene, the tiny ruddy face, the serenity of the mother, who, by the grace of God, had her baby without pain. They were men of such poverty and humility that their colored threadbare cloaks spoke more eloquently than their tongues. Their adoration came from full hearts.

If there was any wonderment in Mary's heart, she did not show it. After a while, the shepherds stood and, in the manner of the Jews, apologized for intruding. They addressed their remarks to Joseph because to speak to Mary would have been immodest. They asked Joseph if he had seen the angels and he said no. They related all that had happened to them in the valley. Joseph shook his head. Mary nodded toward the sleeping baby, as though she and he alone understood that this was only the first of many great world events.

The shepherds left, praising God, and in their joy awakening people to tell them that the promised messiah had come. Everything, they said, had been revealed exactly as the angel in the sky had said it would be. Most of their audience ordered them to go in peace. Thus, if one can say that the place of birth was small, humble, a place of animals and odors, then one can also say that the first apostles were the most humble and scorned of men.

ON THE SAME NIGHT, A BRIGHT star appeared in the eastern sky. It came up majestically over the rim of the world and could be plainly seen through the trees of a forest, in the mirror of a quiet lake, a blue pearl over a tawny desert, a gem of hope far at sea. It was seen by many, and marked by few. The star came up blue-white, in the orderly orbit of the heavens, and it seemed so large that it shed blue shafts of radiance.

Three of the men who studied it were Gaspar, Melchior and Balthasar. They were rich Persians. In the southeast, they regarded the new star in the east and stroked their beards. These were wise men, scholars who were referred to as the Magi and who were known in Persia as philosophers, scientists, astrologists and followers of Zoroastrianism, a creed which fought the worship of graven idols and believed that there was but one God for all men.

The Magi were excited about the star. It had two phases of interest for them. One was the physical—where did this star come from and why had it not appeared in the night sky before? The other was the symbolic: what message was the star trying to convey? The three wise men pondered these things and could come to no agreement on the first premise.

One argued that it was not really a star, but a rare conjunction of two or more stars. This could not be so, a second said, because if it were, their paths, having converged, would soon part and they would be seen as separate stars. A third said that the star was really an unknown comet, appearing brilliantly in the eastern sky, and doomed quickly to pass from view.

Whether it was several stars, or planets, in conjunction, or whether it was a fiery body without a visible tail, the star had special meaning. They were sure of this. They consulted some of the old astrological predictions, and found nothing that would fit the situation. They tried some of the old Greek and Persian tracts, but found nothing which might apply.

It wasn't until they went over the ancient Jewish scriptures that the wise men saw the true meaning of the big star. There was an old prophecy by Balaam which said: "I shall see him, but not now. I shall behold him, but not near. A star shall rise out of Jacob and a scepter shall spring up from Israel."

The star then would mean that a saviour of the Jews had been born. Melchior agreed that, if the star could not be explained in any natural manner, this interpretation was important—to the Jews. Oh no, said Balthasar, more than the Jews because Balaam, the prophet who uttered the words near the end of the forty years' wandering, was not a Jew. He was a gentile. In fact, the words, according to scripture, had been said in the Mountains of Moab, on the edge of Persia—outside of Israel.

If so, said Gaspar, then the fact that the star had been seen by Persians, and properly interpreted by them, would have exciting meaning for the entire world. It was possible that the messiah had come to save not only the Jews, but the Medes, the Assyrians, the Romans, the Babylonians, the savages farther to the east.

At once, the three wise men left their tents, determined to follow the star. They packed food and water, and the special trappings of rich philosophers, and started out on camels to find the place of the King of Kings. None of them expected to reach a destination in one night and there was some disagreement among them about whether the star would appear again on the following night, so that its path could be traced.

Toward dawn, the big star was pale in the western sky and they turned their slow plodding camels toward it. They moved across the sands of the desert, with the rising sun behind them, and they pitched their tents by day, and mounted again when the evening sky turned deep blue and the big star came up again, a brazen gem winking along the rim of sky and earth.

If the portent was correct, and this star foretold the king of the Jews, then it was important to the Magi to see the king, to pay homage, and to bring gifts. The trip occupied several days. They came through the passes of Moab into Jericho, where the Dead Sea and the River Jordan meet, and they crossed the river and went on up into Jerusalem.

On the last night, they seemed to be almost under the big star. At its zenith, it seemed to be almost overhead.

In the early evening, the three august personages went to Solomon's temple and stood, as was required, in the outer Court of the Gentiles. They addressed one of the seven thousand Levitical priests, and asked: "Where is the newborn king of the Jews? It was his star we saw in the East, and we came to offer homage to him."

The Magi appeared to be happy and expectant, but the Levitical priest did not share their joy. He summoned a ranking member of the Sanhedrin, and the Magi explained the new star and their interpretation of the happy sign. The high priest asked questions, frowned, and said that he knew nothing of such a sign. However, as a mark of respect to the rich visitors, he detailed the beliefs of the Jews about the messiah, some of which sounded, to gentile ears, contradictory.

One of the prophecies was:

> Behold! The virgin will be pregnant
> and give birth to a Son,
> Who will be called Emmanuel—
> Which means, God with us.

There were others, the high priest said, one of which mentioned the town of David:

And you, Bethlehem, in the land of Judea,
Are not the least of Judea's principalities;
For out of you shall come forth a Ruler,
Who will shepherd my people Israel.

This, said the wise men, would appear to be the most promising clue because, as they approached Jerusalem, the star was close overhead. Bethlehem, five miles south of the holy city, would be a good place to go. They thanked the high priest, and camped outside the walls for the night. It was decided that, if the new king was not in Bethlehem, the wise men would make a few more inquiries, and then turn homeward.

The high priest was vexed. He knew that the people of Judea set great store by the portents of the stars, and he did not want the ridiculous assumptions of the gentiles to become common knowledge. Suppose there was a baby in Bethlehem? If the Magi found him, and adored him, the people would hear of it and this might turn them away from the great temple of Jerusalem.

He waited until the early watch and stood in the tower over the gold grapes on the east wall of the temple, squinting into the night sky. It appeared that there was no star, and the priest felt relieved. He was about to descend when a bright light appeared to hang between the jagged peaks of Moab. He studied it a moment, waited, and then expelled a long sigh. It was a star. An unusually large star.

The high priest reported to the palace of King Herod and relayed the news. The sovereign was insane. He was a dark, bearded man with wild, rolling eyes and he had been dying of a wasting disease for a year. Herod listened to the news on a couch and ordered the high priest to summon the Magi. He asked their interpretation of the meaning of the big star, and they told him that it should be a joy and comfort to a king so ill to know that, in all probability, God had sent a saviour to take his place.

Herod offered some grapes and figs and asked many questions. He appeared to have an academic interest in the new king—if there was a new king—and he hoped that if the Persian philosophers found the baby, they would do him the courtesy of informing him, so that the king could offer his own tribute to the new majesty. By the way, he said, if the star first appeared when the baby was born we should be able to tell the age of the new king by knowing how long the star has been in the sky.

Melchior shook his head. We saw the star recently, he said, but it was possible that it had been in the sky—perhaps on another path—for many months. We would doubt this, but it was possible.

The three wise men exchanged gifts with Herod and left. At once, the mad king called in the council of the nation—the high priests and the scribes—and he demanded that they interpret the symbolism of the new star, and do something about it at once. He assured them that if, for example, the star was over Bethlehem and some unknown infant was there, the stupid people of the streets would spread the news all over Judea and would desert the temple and, worst of all, their lawful king, in favor of a squalling, whimpering infant.

Some of the high priests favored sending spies to follow the Magi, but Herod was opposed to this. No, he said, I have asked them as a courtesy to return to me with whatever news they may have. I will deal with that situation later. At the moment, I expect you to show some gratitude to the person who rebuilt your temple—me. Spread the news among the faithful that, when the messiah comes, he will come fully grown, on a cloud, attended by legions of trumpeting angels, and he will come directly to the earthly home of his Father—the temple.

No one smiled, but some of the priests must have been tempted.

They were acquainted with Herod's record. He was the cruelest of all kings and, in their opinion, the furthest removed from God and his works. The people had not chosen him as their king. Thirty-five years ago, a Roman emperor had appointed Herod the Great and, for three years, the people of Israel were in rebellion.

Now he had to contend with an unknown baby. After thirty-five years of sovereignty, Herod was dying slowly and dyspeptically, and he could not even undergo that with serenity. A baby intruded. Well, he would await the return of the Magi, and he would deal with the baby in a manner Herod considered to be direct.

ON THE EIGHTH DAY, THE infant was taken to the synagogue in Bethlehem for circumcision. Centuries before, God had commanded Abraham, as part of a convenant, to circumcise all male Jews shortly after birth. It pledged all sons of Judea to observance of the law.

Mary wrapped the baby warmly, and handed him to Joseph. The man took him outside the cave and on up the steep path to the inn. This was the baby's first sight of the world he had come to save and, from his blanket, all he saw was azure-blue sky and sunlight. Up there, somewhere, was the heaven from which he had come and to which he would return only after giving his mortal life in pain.

Joseph passed the inn and went on to the crossroads of Bethlehem. There he saw the synagogue and, after inquiries, took the precious charge inside. He asked the rabbi if he could circumcise the first-born himself. The teacher nodded. Joseph said that he had had no experience with this, and he would need some assistance. The rabbi smiled. He understood. It was common for new fathers to ask to officiate, and it was also common for them to be frightened at the prospect.

The teacher guided the hand of Joseph, and the first few drops of precious blood were shed. So too were the first tears. Symbolically, the young lamb was on the altar. The Son of God was obedient to the law of the Father. The rabbi asked the name to be given the baby and Joseph said Jeshua.* This was the name given to Mary by the archangel. It was also given to Joseph in a dream.

The ancient prophet Isaias had predicted that the name

* "Jeshua" is the Hebrew form for the Greek word "Jesus." It means "God is Saviour" and "God Saves." Christ is not a surname. It is a Greek version of the Hebrew "Mashiah" or "Messiah"—the Anointed. In his public ministry, the Saviour was properly referred to as "Jesus, the Christ."

of the Son of God would be Emmanuel, which means "God with us." He also said that the messiah would be called the Prince of Peace, God the Mighty, Wonderful, Counselor and Father of the World to Come. The only name in which all of these meanings are embraced is Jeshua, or Jesus.

The baby was carried back to the tiny stable, with its loose-board room. Jesus was now an infant Jew; a son of the family of David. He would be uncomfortable for several days, but he had suffered the first pain of the man child, and Joseph patted the bottom of the blanket to soothe him.

THE MAGI WAITED UNTIL the star came up, east of Jerusalem, and then, when it again neared the zenith in the night sky, they mounted their camels, and followed it the final few miles. They started on the north side of Jerusalem, where there was a bazaar for gentiles, and passed the Gate of Damascus and went across the swift-flowing Kidron to a little place called Gethsemani, then south toward the Valley of Himmon and on up the winding road near the field of the potter and straight south to Bethlehem.

The star seemed to move before them, as stars do when

people travel, but when they came to Bethlehem the blue-white gem appeared to be directly overhead. They asked the few pilgrims who still remained after the Roman census if a king had been born in the area. The pilgrims said that they had heard no such news. The wise men tried several places, but the replies to their questions were vague and guarded.

The Magi looked like rich gentiles, which they were, and the people were disinclined to consort with them, even in conversation. It was Gaspar who said that the question should be rephrased. Instead of asking if a king was born, let us ask if a baby has been born.

They tried this tack with no success until they stopped at the inn for refreshment. They were told that an unknown couple from the north had had a baby. No one knew anything about the family. The newborn could be found below, in the stable. The three wise men looked at each other, and wondered. A stable? A king in a stable?

They went outside and again checked the prophecies of the ancient Jews and the portent of the star. The signs, they were forced to conclude, were correct. Balthasar pointed out that there was much evidence that the One

God acts in ways mysterious to man, and that there must be a reason—a reason which escaped them—for having the All Highest born of unknown people in a stall for animals. Gaspar agreed but he spoke for all when he said that, even though the reason appeared to be unfathomable, they had inquired around the town and only one baby had been born and this one must be the one promised by God to the Jews.

Melchior nodded solemnly and the three men pitched a tent outside the inn and removed their traveling garments and changed into raiment befitting their station in life. This was a happy moment for the sophisticated Persians. They had, as a matter of course, been on intimate terms with kings who had sought their counsel. This would be the first majesty who would be an infant and, at the same time, the Anointed of God.

From the saddle pouches, they withdrew their gifts, adorned themselves with the jewelry of their rank, and, in solemn file, walked down the path to the stable. At the entrance to the stony grotto, they were met by Joseph. Gaspar introduced himself and his confreres, and told Joseph that they had come a long way to adore the new king.

The foster father excused himself, and went inside to consult with Mary. In a moment, he was back, asking them to enter, apologizing for the humbleness of his quarters. The Magi did not hear him. They were looking beyond Joseph to Mary, who sat crouched on straw with the infant in her arms. She glanced up briefly, then reverted to what she had been doing: touching downward at the baby's chin to make him smile.

The three wise men threw themselves onto the grain-sanded floor, the folds of their brocaded garments spilling into the chaff. They touched their foreheads to the floor, and announced that they had come to pay homage to the new king. Mary glanced at them tenderly, and held her baby so that they could see his face.

Mary smiled. And the little one smiled. The wise men remained grave. They studied the infant's face as though they were trying to etch it in their memories. Their knees remained on the floor throughout the visit, and when Gaspar felt that it was time to go he nodded to Melchior, who made a formal address about bringing gifts suitable to one who would be referred to as the All Highest.

He reached behind, and brought forth a small ornate

casket. As it was opened, Mary turned to look. Joseph stood in the archway watching. The baby dozed. Melchior opened the casket and announced the gifts of the Magi as they were laid out upon a white cloth. There was a small packet of gold dust. Then a jar of frankincense, a fragrant essence of resins and oils from East Africa, and myrrh, a rare orange-colored gum used as a perfume unguent.

Joseph was abashed. He was a young man from a provincial town, but he realized that these gifts were reserved as a tribute to sovereigns. He tried to express his gratitude, but the words died on the roof of his mouth. Mary smiled and thanked the visitors, and hoped that God would guide them home in safety.

The Magi backed to the door of the stable and left. They decided to spend the night in Bethlehem, and to leave in the morning. Before their little camp they set a fire and sat talking about the visit and the portent to the world represented by the newborn. Balthasar said that he could detect a radiance, an aura of light, around the messiah. Melchior said that he too had noticed. Gaspar was looking at the night sky. What, he asked, happened to that big blue star?

In the night, the Magi were warned not to return to King Herod with the news of finding the messiah. They were not told why. In the morning, the three philosophers agreed that, although it would be wrong to ignore the invitation of Herod to return to Jerusalem, it would be worse to ignore the warning of an angel in a dream. So they packed their tents and utensils, mounted their camels and, instead of returning north to Jerusalem, headed east through Marsaba then north to Jericho and across the Jordan into Peraea.

There was a time of quiet; a time of family communion; a time to think. There were two ceremonies to be undergone before they could go home to Nazareth—the presentation of the first-born at the temple in Jerusalem, and the purification of the mother. The first, under the law, could take place any time after the thirty-first day of a male child. The second could not occur before the forty-first day.

Joseph said that it would not be wise to return to Nazareth and then come back for the visitation to the temple. It would be better to remain in Bethlehem and, on the morning of the forty-first day, to take the child to

Jerusalem, obey the law, and return to the cave and pack up preparatory to leaving for the long trip home the next day.

Altogether, the carpenter would be away from his business for many weeks. This, for a young man who had recently concluded his apprenticeship, was a long time. He must return to his work. In a craft as precarious as his, it was important to remain in good favor with the townsmen and a man could not do that if he was not available for work.

Mary agreed. She was a tractable, obedient wife, a girl whose hours were taken up with her baby. The baths, the feedings, the changes, sitting with him in the early sunlight on the side of the hills, rocking him to sleep and crooning to him in the late hours all tended to confuse the young mother between her son's divinity and his human aspects. He was a baby—her baby—but he was also God, and the daily ministrations to his normal needs moved her mother's heart to dwell upon him as an infant who needed maternal care and love.

But, when the baby slept, and she and Joseph had time to discuss, in whispers, the wondrous things which had happened, and which would come in the future, they were beset by anxiety and they did not know what was expected of them. Joseph seemed at times to have a deeper appreciation of the destiny of the youngster. Mary, on the other hand, had an appreciation of each of the wonders of the birth of the messiah, but seemed unable to group them into one big mural.

It was better this way because, had the Father permitted her to see the enormity of the whole plan, she would have been overwhelmed in the presence of Jesus and could not have discharged the duties of a good mother in the normal intercourse of raising a child. Another factor was that the Son of God had come to earth to be born, to "grow in wisdom and in favor with God and men," to engage in a public ministry to show the true and only way to heaven, and to die in self-willed pain for all men. These things would not have been truly of earth if Jesus had not elected to be as human as his neighbors.

Neither Mary nor Joseph ever lost sight of the real mission of Jesus, nor of his divinity. They knew. In the years ahead there would be many strange and awesome things to remind them, again and again, that the human aspect was a condescension of God to man, whom he created and loved. The divine side would be hidden for more than thirty years and, when it was revealed publicly, it would be done at a marriage feast, and solely to please his mother. The sorrows were still far away.

The first forty-one days were sentimental ones for Mary and Joseph. They were happy ones spent in the humblest surroundings. When the census taking was over, they could have moved up to the inn because there was room, but it would have been an added expense, and Joseph's carpentry in the stable had turned out so well that the young couple felt relaxed and at home among the domestic animals.

At dawn on the forty-first day, Joseph saddled the little jackass, and packed enough food and water for one day's travel. It would be five miles up to Jerusalem and five back. Then, after a good night's rest, they would pack everything, pay the innkeeper, and start the five-day trip to Nazareth.

Jerusalem and its great temple were like a giant hive to the Judean bees who appeared in long dusty lines along the inbound roads in the morning and who, after the last evening sacrifice, left in long slow queues, like thousands of dark insects who, after spawning, leave at a common time without communicating with each other.

In the northbound group, Joseph led the little animal and, on it, Mary and Jesus. He saw the backs of animals and people ahead of him, and he accepted the alkali dust on his lips and the gritty taste between his teeth as a concomitant of travel. The Jews they met were not friendly because it was not considered seemly to exchange greetings. In ordinary conversation, well-educated people averted eyes because it was felt to be immodest to stare into another person's eyes.

Joseph passed the big field of the potter to the south of Jerusalem, walked up the Valley of the Kidron to the north side, and entered the Sheep Gate. He tethered the ass, and took Mary to the Gate of the Women and gave her some coins. Joseph took the baby in his arms and the mother smiled at the awkwardly tender manner in which he held Jesus, and she adjusted the folds of the swaddling clothes so that the sun would not hit the baby's eyes.

The foster father first walked out into the courtyard and bought two turtledoves for sixteen cents. This was called the offering of the poor. A proper offering would have been a lamb, but the price of unblemished lambs on the temple grounds was seventy-five cents. In a land where the average family income probably did not exceed fifty dollars, Joseph could not afford anything but the most modest sacrifice.

The mother stood timidly in the area reserved for the women of Israel. She saw many other women, of all ages, worshiping. Then she heard the high, thin wail of the organ, which announced that incense was to be kindled on the Golden Altar. This summoned all women who had recently given birth to infants, and who had come to the temple to be purified.

Ahead of Mary were huge trumpets standing on end, their wide mouths standing like golden lilies against the marble of the house of God. She recalled Joseph's instructions and into one of these she dropped her offering for the sacrifice. She walked up the fifteen steps to the Nicanor Gate. There were other young women with her. On the far side of the gate was the Court of Israelite Men, and females were not allowed there.

The station men of the temple met the young women and assisted in the sacrifices, the burnt offerings, the sin offerings, the drink offerings, and as the incense floated up into the blue morning sky the hymn of praise, *Tris-Hagion,* filled the cold corridors. Afterward, Mary was levitically clean, pure of stain, and could participate in sacred offerings. She rejoined Joseph and Jesus.

Joseph took the baby into the sacrificial section of the temple. The presentation ceremony was, in effect, a buying back of a son. The first-born, under Jewish law, was reserved for God. He must be free of such bodily blemishes as would bar him from the priesthood and, on his thirty-first day or after, the father must first offer the male son to God, then redeem him from a priest. The cost was high—about $2.50.

The young carpenter gave the baby to a priest, who accepted him with practiced hands, and, as he turned toward the altar, an old man named Simeon peered into the folds protecting the baby's face, and at once fell back, shielding his eyes. He emitted a cry which attracted attention, and Joseph, concerned for his son, also looked into the folds of the swaddling to make certain that Jesus was all right. Mary clasped her hands and closed her eyes.

The old man was a devout and conscientious Jew who had done many good works in his life. He longed for the promise of redemption by God, and his longing was so poignant that the Holy Spirit had revealed to Simeon that he would not die until he had been permitted to see the messiah.

Because of this, Simeon had attended the presentation of male sons every morning for many years, waiting for the promise to be fulfilled. He had grown old waiting. The daily inspection of infants by Simeon had made him, in the eyes of some priests, a pest. Now, for the first time, he had looked at one more baby's face and had fallen back as though blinded.

Joseph did not know him, nor the story of the promise. Before anyone could stop Simeon, he took Jesus from the arms of the priest and, with aged eyes on the morning sky, crooned a hymn to God.

> "Now," he sang, "you may release
>   your bondsman, O Master,
>   according to your promise,
>   in Peace!
>   For my eyes have looked upon the salvation
>   which you have prepared
>   for all the nations to behold,
>   a Light to illumine the Gentiles,
>   a Glory to grace your people Israel."

The priests and the communicants listened in wonder. Mary opened her eyes and saw at once that this was another in a long chain of divine manifestations. She looked so kindly into the face of the old man that Simeon handed the baby back to the priest, and turned to Mary with tears in his eyes.

> "Alas!" he said to her. "This babe is destined
> to be the downfall no less
> than the restoration of many in Israel!
> His very name will provoke contradiction,
> and your own soul, also,
> shall be pierced by a sword!
> And thus the secret thoughts of many a heart
> shall be laid bare."

This was the first that Mary knew that, in her selection as the mother of God, there would be sorrow and tragedy. If, as seems likely, she thought that her enormous honor would carry with it nothing but the pleasant task of bringing the infant up in righteousness to do the will of the Father, she was mistaken. She was beginning to learn that the work of the messiah was a study in contrasts.

STADELSCHES KUNSTINSTITUT, FRANKFORT

Adoration of the Shepherds
Martin Schongauer (ca. 1430–1491)

GALLERIA DEGLI UFFIZI, FLORENCE

Adoration of the Magi (*detail*)
Gentile da Fabriano (*ca. 1370–1427*)

He was God, but he had chosen to be born in the humblest abode. Still, his advent had been heralded by angels from Heaven. His mother was a poor, unknown virgin and his foster father was a poverty-stricken carpenter, but rich wise men had come, unannounced, out of the east to adore the baby. Now, in the holiest place in all Israel, an old man had stepped forth to state, without blasphemy, that this child was the salvation of the world. Who told him? she wondered. How did the old man know? And what did he mean by saying that her soul would be pierced by a sword?

She was meditating on these things when a commotion arose and out of the crowd came the oldest-looking woman Mary had ever seen. Her face was a skeleton over which saffron skin was stretched. The woman dragged her legs forward, toward the infant, and no one tried to stop her. The priests acknowledged her presence by bowing curtly. This was Anna, the prophetess. She was the daughter of Phanuel of the tribe of Aser, and she was known as one of the holiest of women.

Anna had married young and, for seven years, had been happy. Her husband had been taken from her suddenly, and she had turned to God and the great temple. She was there every morning; she was there every evening. She had been a widow for eighty-four years and, counting the seven years of marriage, and the ritualistic age of fifteen before marriage, the prophetess was probably one hundred and six years of age.

When she had dragged her ancient frame to the side of Jesus, she peered at him, and turned away, thanking God over and over. From that day on, she went among the women at the temple, preaching about Jesus to all who hoped for the redemption of Israel.

Order was restored in the temple, and the baby was presented to the Lord. He was found to be without blemish. Joseph redeemed him with money and with a sacrificial offering of the doves. The sun was hardly at its zenith when Joseph led his spouse and the baby back to where the jackass was tethered.

Joseph took another look at the baby, to see if he could see anything unusual—any radiance, perhaps—which might have moved the old man and the old lady in the temple. What he saw was a round face, dark ringleted hair, clear olive skin, and red lips pouting a little in sleep.

He saw a baby.

THE LITTLE FAMILY WAS ready to return to Nazareth when Joseph awakened the next morning early and sat in silence until Mary opened her eyes. She saw the frown and asked if he was troubled. Yes, he said, he was. In the night he had had a dream. He saw an angel, the same one he had seen before. The angel was agitated. "Rise!" he commanded. "Take with you the child and his mother and flee into Egypt! Remain there until I give you further notice. Herod is on the point of searching for the child in order to take his life!"

The young foster father looked appealingly to his wife. Should he heed the dream, or should they return home? Mary had no doubt about the course they should pursue. They must hurry to Egypt. If an angel ordered this, then God had told the angel to do it. But how, Joseph asked, could Herod himself be aware of the baby Jesus? It did not matter, Mary said. They must follow the commands of God without question, and this was a command.

Joseph realized that Mary was right. He was so proud of his little family, and so homesick, that he had hoped to start the journey to Nazareth at once, and he did not like having to move further away—to an alien land. Joseph paid the innkeeper that day, and bought some food for the saddlebag, and stocked up with water.

He told no one that he was leaving, or in which direction he would travel when he did. That night, Mary wrapped her baby carefully against the chill air, set her cloak around her slender body, and took a last look at the little stable and the animals who had remained so strangely quiet for so many days. In the faint evening light, the goats and a ewe and a thin cow turned liquid eyes on her.

Joseph had knocked down the stall boards which formed the little room, and had set them back where they belonged. He looked weary. When the blue dark of night set in, Mary mounted the little ass, held her baby against her breast, and the young man yanked the halter strap and started to plod along the white-stoned road south to Egypt.

It seemed strange to Joseph, walking toward the great desert, that anyone would want to hurt a baby. Any baby. It seemed even stranger that God was keeping this one a secret. The only ones who knew that this tiny jostled, sleeping burden behind him was the Son of God were the despised and poor shepherds of the fields, and the despised and rich gentiles from Persia. The king of all Judea, Herod the Great, had heard about the infant Jesus, and his reaction, according to the angel, was to plot a murder.

Now, they could not even take their happiness home. They had to travel all the way to Bethlehem to have the baby and must travel hundreds of miles further from home to save the baby's life. They were in flight to spare an infant who had come to save the souls of all mankind.

Why? Joseph begged to understand.

THE KING'S PALACE WAS A place of splendid courtyards and many oil lamps on the west side of Jerusalem, about three hundred yards from a place called Golgotha, or Calvary. Men of importance were rushing, on this night, in and out of the palace. Herod the Great was in a towering rage. He arose from his couch, a man with deepset eyes like caves in a forest, and his gray beard parted and his tongue spat words. Many, he said, would pay for the trick which had been played upon him. Many would die. His courtiers trembled because, if the lives of his loved ones could be sacrificed at a whim, their lives were less than worthless.

Spies had come to him from several quarters. The first ones said that the Magi had remained in Bethlehem two days and had left for Persia, skirting Jerusalem to the south. This showed that they had no intention of keeping their promise to return to the king with news of the newborn messiah. Other spies had been sent at once to Bethlehem to find the baby and his parents and bring them to the august presence of Herod. But these had returned with bad news indeed: the little family, it seemed, had lived in a stable beneath the inn, and both stable and inn were now empty.

Herod's soldiers had arrested the innkeeper and his wife, but torture could bring no further information than that they had no room at the inn for the expectant mother, and had permitted her to live in the stable with her husband and newborn. The king was seventy years of age, and very ill, but his rage enslaved him and he tore fabrics and drapes from the walls and screamed until the saliva hung on his beard.

The census, he roared. That would provide a solution to the problem of the make-believe messiah who had come to exact tribute from the gullible Jews. The census. He called an aide and ordered him to go to the Roman tribune now in quarters at Fortress Antonia and to ask in the name of the king for the names of all families who had infants.

The aide was about to run outdoors when Herod stopped him. Wait, he screamed. Wait or I will fix it so that you will not be able to run anywhere. We must first find out how old this particular baby is. Call my councilors!

The learned ones came in, their striped cloaks betraying the trembling of men underneath. How long, said Herod, had that accursed star been in the sky? No one knew. They had not looked for a star. Herod moaned and sobbed and pounded the wall with his withered fists. If the Magi could see such a star, why cannot my councilors see it? Can it be that my learned assistants are in league with the little one who aspires to usurp my throne?

The soothsayers said that the strange bright star could not have been in the heavens long, or else astrologers among the Jews would have broadcast the news. They would also have made their own dire predictions about it. This, they reasoned, made it likely that the star was on a path across Persia toward Bethlehem and that it had begun its flight recently.

A year ago? shouted Herod. A week ago? I must find out the age of his little majesty. The councilors looked at each other and said surely no more than a year. Probably far less. Herod the Great leaned his hands on his couch and gasped for air. Then, he said, I know what to do. I know what to do. He punched the couch arm with his hand.

He sent the courier to the Roman tribune. He was to ask, in the name of the king, for a list of all Jewish families who had male sons two years of age or less. The census would reveal the status of every family—how many members, what age. When the list was copied, he wanted it given to his chief of guards and he wanted squads of soldiers sent to Bethlehem, Jerusalem and every town and village in the area. The soldiers were under orders from the king to tear the babies from their parents and to either kill them on the spot with the short sword, or take them out in batches and cast them from the cliffs.

One councilor coughed politely and asked if it wouldn't be more prudent to kill only those babies up to the age of one, and only those who were born of the family of David in the town of Bethlehem.

Herod shrieked. He held his fists against the sides of his head and rocked with pain. When he again caught his breath, he said the order was to kill all babies from the age of one hour to the age of two years, and this would include all babies in the vicinity of Bethlehem. There would be no exemptions, even among the babies of the soldiers themselves. This must be done at once, so that no spurious pretender to the throne could grow up and lift the scepter from Herod's cold hands.

In fact, while he thought about the matter, Herod the Great dwelled upon the idea of killing his own son, Herod Antipas. He too aspired to this throne, the throne on which none but the one Herod, the true Herod, the Great Herod, would sit. He said nothing at the moment, but mentally marked his son for death within the week.

Within a few days, the slaughter of the innocents began. Soldiers in squads hurried from house to house, tearing babies from the arms of screaming mothers, throwing them on earthen floors and running short swords through the little bodies. In every village, anguish and wailing followed the running visit of death. In Jerusalem, some bereft mothers tried to carry their dead infants into the temple, as sacrifices.

No newborn babies were killed in Bethlehem, because only one had been born there in the past year. Older ones were killed, and some were cast from the cliffs down into the valley of the shepherds. In Jerusalem, some of Herod's soldiers wept because they had to kill the babies of fellow soldiers. All up to the age of two were slain because to fail by one baby would have brought death to many soldiers.

Some of the elders shook their heads sadly and wiped their eyes as they remembered the old words of the prophet Jeremias:

> "A cry was heard at Rama,
>   there was weeping and sore lament.
>   Rachel wept for her children;
>   She would not be consoled,
>   because they were no more."

The news mollified King Herod. He asked many questions about the killings, and was pleased that his officers had done an efficient job. Surely the so-called baby king was among the many who died in the swift raids. There was no chance that any infant had escaped the holocaust. There were weeping and mourning all over the land and only Herod was happy.

For a while, his peace of mind improved his health. To celebrate this feeling of tranquillity, the king ordered his son Antipater to be executed at once. When this was done, Herod felt even better because now there was no one in all the nation who aspired to his throne.

He was, for a time, almost benevolent. The king began to eat again and managed to feel a little surge of joy at sight of the rising sun. Then he was seized with a fit, and fell to the floor of his palace. His councilors and officers were summoned and they stood around in a little group and watched the king strangle slowly. There was nothing they could do to help him, and, apparently, there was no wish to ameliorate his last hour.

They stood polite and mute in the presence of majesty, and watched him grovel and tear at his throat, the dark eyes bulging from his head, a plea for assistance in the dying eyes. When Herod's final gasp subsided in a gasp of resignation, the councilors moved to inform the nation, and Caesar Augustus in Rome, that the king was dead.

He had followed the infants, but he did not join them.

The holy family had been in Egypt a short while when Joseph had another visitation. The young man had found work as an assistant carpenter and, even though he felt unclean in this alien land, his son was growing and beginning to recognize him. His wife was content to be with her baby.

The angel said: "Rise! Take with you the child and his mother, and set out for the land of Israel. They who were plotting against the life of the child are dead." Joseph told Mary, and she prepared their little sack of belongings. Her spouse fetched the food and the water, and they started back across the great desert to Israel.

It was a long, lonely walk for Joseph. He led the little jackass, with its precious burden, over the never-ending dunes which climbed in hilly ridges, sometimes blowing the stinging sand in his young, worried face, sometimes lying still and slippery underfoot, like mountains of brown sugar. His deeply tanned legs had carried him a long, long way, and all because of a baby that wasn't truly his.

The youthful carpenter would have blushed if anyone had called him noble, but he was noble beyond the calling of any man. No love of a man for a woman had been put to such spirit-breaking tests as this one, and survived in unquestioning meekness. If he had felt so disposed, he could have passed the visitations of the angel off as wishful dreams. He could have banished his bride, had her stoned to death, or, at the least, had her sent off to a faraway place to have her baby in loneliness and sorrow.

He sustained all of the trials, and it dizzied his mind to think that, for all his remaining days, he would be on special trial before the eyes of God. Then too, although he had committed no crime, he was forced to flee hundreds of miles to Egypt, and now, in some trepidation, he was going back to his homeland, perhaps to face arrest and sudden death.

There was lots of time to think, because walking in the heavy, cloying sand was slow, hot work. With each step, the sandals shed a cascade of dry tan grains and the brassy sun soaked his garments until the sweat ran down his legs. Joseph had lots of time to think.

There was another side to his life. A side which repaid him, and more, for all the sacrifices. He, of all the men in the world, had been chosen to be the paternal guardian of the Christ. He could not think of a reason why he had been selected for this enormous honor, but he would discharge it within the framework of the laws of God.

He had already made up his mind about the future. The family would return home. He would take up his work as carpenter as though nothing had happened except that, in the census at Bethlehem, his wife had given birth to a baby. Joseph would say nothing about the divinity of the child unless he was so ordered by another visitation.

The best thing for the baby, he figured, was a normal upbringing. He hoped that Mary would not oppose him in this. And he hoped too that their knowledge of the child's sacredness would not influence them in his daily care. He would not want Jesus to get special treatment. Joseph enjoyed the laughter and play of youngsters, and it was not too long ago that he had squatted in the dirt streets of Nazareth playing games with the boys. Still, laughter and play implied discipline, and he might have to be firm with Mary, so that she would be firm with the child.

The best way would be to raise the boy as Joseph had been raised. When he had asked permission to do something, his parents often said no. It would have to be that way with this one. The law of the land said that, between the ages of one and five, the male child should be taught the fundamental truths about God and the law. This work was imposed on the mother.

So Mary would have to teach. She would impart the ancient truths orally, as all mothers did in Judea. The boy would have to pay attention and, in time, be able to recite the ancient wisdom in Hebrew. At the age of five, he would be ready to attend daily classes at the synagogue. There, the lessons would be more advanced, and the rabbi would brook no horseplay among the boys. He would expect them to know a great deal about the law before they left their mothers' sides. One must start to teach the child, Joseph figured, as soon as he was able to comprehend.

It would be awkward, teaching God about God, but Joseph's simple, direct mind calculated that, if the messiah had chosen to be born of humble people in a stable, then he would not, at the age of one or two, begin to speak in mystical enigmas. He would probably choose to live as Joseph had ordained.

If that was so, Joseph was pleased. He would, in time, teach Jesus how to square a piece of lumber and cut it;

how to cut a dowel and insert it in cypress; how to make use of small scraps of wood in a land almost denuded of lumber; how to care for a little donkey and to load it with a day's work; how to be respectful to a mother even when he disagreed with her wishes.

He would enjoy teaching the boy to be a man. The more he thought about it, the happier Joseph became. His feet no longer seemed heavy as he walked in the sand. When he passed the big caravans, heading south from Jerusalem, he managed a small smile and a wave at the camel drivers.

Joseph couldn't average more than ten miles a day. In the evening, he looked for a high dune, and stopped in the lee of it, out of the wind, and helped Mary and the baby down. He apportioned the water, drew the dry sticks from the saddlebag for the fire, and gave his spouse the privacy she and the infant needed until the food was ready.

Sometimes, in the evening, Mary's arms were so fatigued with cradling the baby all day that she wept as she rubbed them to restore circulation. The baby was placed on a mound of sand, and the little cotton hood shielded his face as his mother helped with the evening work. She drew extra blankets from beneath the saddle of the donkey. The nights on the desert were bone-chilling and Joseph could not keep the fire going because the ass could not carry enough wood to get them across the desert.

To Mary, Joseph became more precious by the hour because she understood his nobility and his sacrifice. She knew that her own burdens would be heavy—heavier, in time, than his—but hers were counterbalanced by the tremendous joy of having been chosen to be the mother of God. Also, she had the physical presence of the baby, and the attendant maternal joy of ministering to him, watching him grow stronger day by day, feeding him, changing him, and doing the scores of things a young mother enjoys doing for her own precious baby.

The mother wasn't much more than a baby, but she was competent, as all the young women of the land were, and wise in the ways of motherhood. All of them had been brought up with little formal knowledge beyond religion, the law, and how to take care of a home and a family. The child fell into this mode of life as gracefully as though she had never been intended for anything else—as indeed she hadn't.

The thing which marred her ecstatic happiness was

Herod. Mary was terrified at the mention of his name. She could not understand why anyone would take the life of a baby—any baby—least of all hers. Her fair chin trembled with mute fright whenever she thought of the possibility of losing the world's most precious burden, but then, to her surprise, she found that terror cannot live long in the human heart.

The human mind will not sustain it. Fright withered and died, and she became occupied with the infant, turning away now and then to think of how lucky she was to have a man like Joseph. At these times, Mary's heart sang with happiness. Already, she had everything good that a young lady could desire, and she had been married less than a year. Even if her precious little lamb had not been the messiah, she would have loved him to distraction. He was hers to fondle, to keep, to talk to even when he could not understand the words, to gaze upon lovingly, to dwell upon in the long hours of the hot sun, to plan for, to raise as her very own.

Hers was the great sustaining happiness. It was not given to her to see any sorrow ahead, any tragedy, as it is not given to any mother to see. Nothing, except Herod, was allowed to quiet the symphony of ecstasy which raced through every fiber of her being, which swelled and kept swelling until she crooned aloud to her baby on the swaying donkey and her Joseph turned, smiling a little, to look upon a sweet face, dark with the dust of the desert, except for little rings around the mouth and eyes.

As they approached Judea and the neat, white little towns, Mary's happiness grew greater because she could see no cause for alarm in her own people. They spoke the same tongue, enjoyed the same life, and the women at the village wells smiled shyly and wished the young stranger well with her baby. The older women insisted on peeling back the little hood and taking a look, as though it were the right of older ones to gaze critically upon the work of the younger ones.

Some admitted grudgingly that the little boy looked plump, and had good color, and advised soft, nourishing cereals to make him grow faster. Mary listened respectfully to her elders, and exchanged small chitchat with the younger women at the well, and sat on a big stone, spread a cloth over her knees, and undressed her little boy and bathed him in the warm Judean sun.

These, for Mary, were the happy days, the days which would sustain her in the years to come. She would remember them, mystically, nostalgically down the corridors of time, and no matter how big her son grew she would remember him as a small, helpless infant who made cooing sounds, and flapped his arms and legs when he was bathed on her knees.

The holy family moved on, day by day, toward the city of David, where all of this had started. Mary's serenity was infectious, and Joseph stopped worrying about the future and spent more time in the evening with his little boy. Mary taught him how to hold a baby, how to change the clothing, how to make him smile, how to hold him over the shoulder after feeding and to pat his back gently until the stomach gases, but not the food, were expelled. The family was now a happy unit.

They were south of Bethlehem when, in the evening, Joseph struck up a conversation with some Jews who had just left Bethlehem. He heard, for the first time, the details of the death of Herod, and he was disturbed to learn that a son called Archelaus was now on Herod's throne.

This worried Joseph, although it did not seem to impress Mary. He told her that he was now afraid to go through Jerusalem. They might be seen. Anyone who might see the tiny burden would wonder why he had not been killed with the others. Someone might report it to the king. Mary thought about it. She said she would defer to Joseph's judgment.

The young foster father took a trail eastward, skirting Bethlehem, and moved on by stages to Jericho, then north to Nazareth. There, among the families of Joseph and Mary, the infant Jesus was safe, and grew in strength and wisdom.

About the Author

Jim Bishop is the originator of "The Day" style of journalism. In his early book, *The Day Lincoln Was Shot,* he proved that an old story can induce unbearable tension in a reader by a recitation of all the little chips of facts leading to the event. He says he got the idea for this style of writing from his father, a police lieutenant who wrote his reports on crime in infinite detail and by the clock.

The author was born in Jersey City, N.J., in 1907. He was educated at St. Patrick's School and Drake's Secretarial College. Bishop's first editorial position was as copy boy on the *News,* in New York. Later, a columnist named Mark Hellinger took him to the *Daily Mirror.* Jim Bishop has held most of the city room jobs, from reporter to caption writer to bulldog editor.

In 1943, he was appointed war editor of *Collier's* and later executive editor of *Liberty* magazine. For a time, he was a literary agent and, in the early 1950's, founding editor of Gold Medal Books. His last editorial position was executive editor of *Catholic Digest.*

He is the author of eleven books and writes a syndicated newspaper column for King Features Syndicate. He has two daughters, Mrs. Charles Frechette and Miss Gail Bishop, and four grandchildren. Bishop is a widower and lives in a house called On The Rocks, Sea Bright, N.J.

THE HOLY LAND
IN THE
TIME OF CHRIST

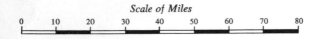

Scale of Miles

0   10   20   30   40   50   60   70   80

MEDITERRANEAN

NILE RIVER

EGYPT